MEDIATION IN ACTION
RESOLVING COURT DISPUTES WITHOUT TRIAL

Hazel Genn is Professor of Socio-Legal Studies in the Law Faculty at University College, London. Professor Genn has a long-standing interest in access to justice and civil litigation and has published widely on these subjects. Her previous publications include *Hard Bargaining* (OUP 1988), *Personal Injury Compensation: How Much is Enough?* (Law Commission 1994), *Survey of Litigation Costs for the Woolf Inquiry into Access to Justice* (LCD 1996), *Understanding Civil Justice* (OUP 1997). She is currently completing work on two national surveys in England/Wales and in Scotland concerning access to justice and public use of courts and alternative dispute resolution.

MEDIATION IN ACTION
RESOLVING COURT DISPUTES WITHOUT TRIAL

HAZEL GENN

FOREWORD BY
THE RIGHT HONOURABLE THE LORD WOOLF MR

CALOUSTE GULBENKIAN FOUNDATION, LONDON

Published by the
Calouste Gulbenkian Foundation
United Kingdom Branch
98 Portland Place
London W1N 4ET
Tel: 0171 636 5313

ISBN 0 903319 85 3
British Library Cataloguing-in-Publication Data
A catalogue record for this book is available from the British Library

Designed by Chris Hyde
Printed by Expression Printers Ltd, IP23 8HH

Distributed by Turnaround Publisher Services Ltd,
Unit 3, Olympia Trading Estate, Coburg Road,
Wood Green, London N22 6TZ. Tel: 0181 829 3000

Cover photograph: Clasped hands, Tony Stone Images.

Contents

Author's Acknowledgements

I would like to pay tribute to His Honour Judge Neil Butter QC of the Central London County Court without whose vision and determination the mediation scheme at the Court would not have been established. The scheme also benefited from a dedicated group of court staff who worked hard to make it a success. Although it tends to be invidious to single out individuals, it is important to record Ginny Melville's enormous contribution to the design of the scheme's administration.

Many members of the public, solicitors and mediators gave freely of their time to assist in the research. Their frank accounts of experiences of disputes and mediation bring the process alive.

At the Gulbenkian Foundation I would like to thank Ben Whitaker for seeing the value in distilling some of the lessons of the CLCC mediation scheme into a widely accessible book, and for his insightful comments on the text. Felicity Luard's skilful editorial work improved the text enormously and I am grateful to her for that.

Finally, I would like to record my deep thanks to my assistant Helen Ghosh at University College London who, as always, provided invaluable assistance and support throughout.

Hazel Genn

Preface

Mediation is being increasingly widely appreciated and used as the preferable solution for many disputes, not merely because the cost of Civil Legal Aid in the UK has risen by 35 per cent over the last five years to £793 million, but because of the great advantages it offers over former legal proceedings in saving time and expense. In addition, a mediation approach almost always results in the parties ending by being more satisfied and less antagonistic than when battle lines have been hardened by the impersonal jousting of litigation and traditional court proceedings – a valuable consideration if, for example, they have to continue living as neighbours.

Similar benefits are equally being recognised in the field of matrimonial disputes, where the new Family Act is encouraging greater use of mediation (which will be free for couples who qualify for Legal Aid), and research has shown that compulsory 'information' meetings for people intending divorce are capable of saving many marriages.

At a time when the number of disputes and cases are likely to grow – especially after the 1998 Human Rights Act applies – Alternative Dispute Resolution is increasingly likely to be used. The Gulbenkian Foundation is particularly pleased to have commissioned and published this book, based on a very encouraging pilot project in mediation at a London court, in order to give a wider number of lay people as well as lawyers the opportunity to learn about mediation's positive advantages.

Ben Whitaker
Director, UK Branch, Calouste Gulbenkian Foundation

Foreword

It should be the primary aim of those involved in civil disputes to avoid going to court except as a last resort. This is a message that the courts should promote. The message is supported by the new Civil Procedures Rules which enable parties to obtain the information they need to assess the validity of claims without having to commence proceedings. It will also be possible under the new Civil Procedure Rules to obtain a stay of legal proceedings to explore the possibility of disposing of the proceedings by Alternative Dispute Resolution (ADR).

There are a variety of methods of ADR which in other jurisdictions have proved their worth. Mediation, which can take different forms, is probably the most effective method of resolving disputes without trial. Unfortunately in the United Kingdom there is still an understandable resistance to taking advantage of what mediation can offer. This is largely based on lack of experience and knowledge of how mediation works and as to how to identify those disputes that are most likely to respond to mediation. This is why I very much welcome this book. The research in which Professor Genn has been involved means that she has an unrivalled knowledge of the mediation process. She is the ideal person to provide the information which lawyers and others engaged in resolving disputes need. By setting out how mediation works, what it can offer and how it can be arranged, this book should prove a valuable resource for anyone interested in the quick, cheap and constructive resolution of disputes.

The Right Honourable The Lord Woolf
Master of the Rolls

Introduction

Although the use of mediation to resolve civil disputes has been gradually growing in popularity over the last few years, it is still a very new process in the UK. It is not generally well understood among the general public, advice agencies, or the legal profession. The use of mediation is very likely to grow in the future, in order to avoid some of the disadvantages of court proceedings and partly in an attempt to cut the expanding cost of Legal Aid.

This book offers practical guidance in simple terms about what is involved in mediation in civil disputes, when it can be used and what its advantages might be over traditional court-based methods of dealing with legal disputes. Drawing on a study of cases recently successfully mediated at a special scheme in the Central London County Court, this book provides insights into the experience of using mediation, and into the potential of mediation as a method of resolving disputes.

Alternative Dispute Resolution (ADR) is arousing increasing interest in the UK and elsewhere. It is hoped that the book will be useful to all those who find themselves involved in legal disputes, whether as private individuals or businesses, and to those who provide advice about how best to deal with legal disputes.

CHAPTER 1

DEALING WITH DISPUTES

Disputes are, unfortunately, a fact of life. We are all at some time or another caught up in disagreements that involve legal rights, whether it is a misleading holiday brochure, a difficult neighbour, or getting the landlord to carry out essential repairs or a supplier to replace a faulty washing machine. Mostly we do not resort to the courts to sort out such problems. But if we fail to resolve them ourselves, or if a

---

Double-glazing disaster

'We signed a contract to install windows. The windows were defective and needed to be replaced. We specified the units we wanted but they put in the wrong units. The original windows they made were too small. They remade them but then they made them too long and too wide. They didn't do what we wanted for heat and noise insulation. We paid £3,000 plus VAT. The window people said it was a matter of "mere" remedial work. They made 16 visits and you can still see light through the edge of the windows. So we don't want them to do any more work. We want someone else. They've been intransigent. They wouldn't answer my phone calls. I said I would go to court and they did nothing. This is a rip-off.'

Late delivery of faulty equipment

'Our suppliers were very late in delivering the machinery and so we were late in completing a job we were doing for someone else. As a result we had to pay a penalty of about £10,000 for late completion. Some of the machine parts were not working and we got no help from the suppliers to fix the problem. We had to repair the machinery ourselves and so we want to recover the cost of the repairs from them and get back the money that we had to pay as a penalty. We have lost contracts as a result of their poor workmanship.'

---

solicitor acting on our behalf fails to do so, then the next step is to get a judge to decide which party is in the right, who should pay whom, and how much. This is, of course, what the courts are there for – to bring disputes to an end and to ensure that ordinary people can enforce their rights.

Three-track system in the courts

Under the new Civil Procedure Rules introduced to the county courts and High Court in 1999, civil claims are now going to be dealt with on different court 'tracks'. There is a 'small claims track' for most cases of less than £5,000 (previously cases of less than £3,000 could

---

Noisy neighbours

'I was being woken up twice every night by my neighbour. He went out in a big diesel van at about 1.00 am and came back at about 5.30 am. I was getting so stressed that I couldn't get to sleep at all. I went over to speak to him one evening and asked him if he could park his van further away from my house. He just said "No". I couldn't believe he could be so unreasonable. We phoned the council but they didn't think there was much they could do. We sent him a solicitor's letter, but he just wrote back saying he had to keep the van outside his house in case it got broken into. It's very difficult to have a war with neighbours. I did think of slashing his tyres. I also considered moving house, which would have been a very drastic step. The thing is it would be so easy to solve the problem, but he just isn't interested.'

The holiday from hell

'The whole holiday was a nightmare...including the train journey from France to Spain. We had been away previously on a similar train journey and had fabulous service and lovely conditions. On this train it was filthy, they didn't serve any food at all. The toilets and water didn't work. We had to find our own luggage and only had a paper sheet to cover ourselves at night. It was so bad we had to buy flights home even though my husband and another of our party are terrified of flying.'

---

be dealt with by the small claims procedure), a 'fast track' for cases over £5,000 (and for personal injury and housing claims over £1,000) and a 'multi-track' for cases over £15,000. The small claims track remains a simple process in which a District Judge decides the case in his room with the parties sitting around a table, usually without lawyers being present. The fast track has fuller procedures but a strict timetable will be imposed. Cases are likely to get to trial faster than previously, and trials will not usually last for more than half a day. The multi-track is only for the most expensive and complicated cases. These will be closely managed by judges to make sure that work on them is done promptly.

The disadvantages of court action

This new system for dealing with civil cases is intended to speed up the process and to reduce the amount that people have to pay to their lawyers, if they use them. However, even though it is likely to improve the way that disputes are dealt with in court, there will always be disadvantages to taking court action. For example, although the small claims procedure is much less daunting than having a case decided in open court, the thought of any kind of hearing before a judge can be somewhat intimidating. And taking legal advice to help resolve a legal problem might turn out to be expensive if it involves going to court, since it can still take quite a long time to prepare a case for trial. Equally importantly, if the people involved in a dispute are going to have to continue to deal or work with each other in the future – for instance, landlords and tenants, neighbours or business associates – then long-drawn-out court litigation is more likely to scupper the relationship than heal the rift. So what is the alternative? Your kitchen is still not finished, you are no longer speaking to the builder, and he doesn't reply to letters from your solicitor. What can you do next?

Concern about these disadvantages of court litigation has led a number of people and organisations, here and abroad, to develop ways of resolving legal disputes without a formal court hearing, protracted delay or the need for expensive lawyers. Such processes are known collectively as Alternative Dispute Resolution or ADR, and an important part of the recent changes to the system of dealing with civil disputes in the courts has been to try and encourage people to solve their problem by ADR rather than by going to trial.

What is Alternative Dispute Resolution?

There are a number of different voluntary ADR processes, such as arbitration, early neutral evaluation, conciliation and mediation.

Arbitration is a private process in which an expert arbitrator, chosen by the disputing parties, hears both sides of the dispute and provides a decision that is quicker, less formal and less expensive than a court hearing. This kind of procedure is often used in business disputes where those involved want the matter to be dealt with privately and by someone with special expertise in the subject matter of the dispute.

SOME JUDGES CAN BE INTIMIDATING

Early neutral evaluation is a process in which a neutral evaluator who has legal or other expertise hears the core of evidence from the parties or their legal representatives at an early stage in the case. Having listened to the basic evidence, the evaluator offers a frank assessment of the strengths and weaknesses of each side's case in the hope that this will lead to a settlement between the parties without further litigation.

Conciliation is a process in which a conciliator takes a proactive approach to try and bring about a settlement and may offer a view on the merits of the dispute. It is intended to be a swift, practical and economic alternative to legal proceedings and is regarded as being particularly effective in complicated disputes that involve more than two parties

Mediation is one of the most commonly used ADR techniques. It is a voluntary process where a neutral mediator attempts to help the disputing parties to reach an agreement that is acceptable to both sides and that will bring the dispute to an early conclusion without having to go to court. A mediator – unlike a judge or an arbitrator – does not have any authority to decide on the issues or to force the parties to reach an agreement. Mediators view disputes as problems that need to be solved in a practical but definitive way, rather than emphasising strict legal rights, and their objective is to bring about a settlement (and a binding agreement), or at least make the key issues clearer. They will discuss each party's grievances, interests, and priorities, to see where there is scope for compromise and to help the parties move towards a settlement that both find acceptable. Organisations that conduct mediations claim that in a very high proportion of cases a dispute can be settled at the end of the mediation session or very soon afterwards.

What are the advantages of mediation?

'Mediation...makes you realise that in a court of law things aren't black and white, and being right doesn't mean you will win...you can still lose your costs.' (Satisfied user of court mediation service.)

Flexibility Mediation is flexible. It can be used for disputes over very large and very small sums of money, or for disputes that do not involve money at all but are concerned with relationships or behaviour, including, for example, those within families or between neighbours. Mediation is often used very successfully in disputes between businesses, and in disputes between tenants and landlords.

Creative agreements Mediation can achieve more creative solutions to disputes than would be possible through court proceedings. Decisions by judges are generally limited to providing financial compensation for things that have happened in the past; mediated agreements can include decisions about what might happen in the future. They can also involve forms of compensation that do not require the payment of money: for example, mutual agreements about future behaviour, a written apology, an explanation of what took place, or an agreement to conduct an investigation.

Repairing relationships Parties in dispute may find it difficult to talk to each other and have trouble in moving towards any kind of compromise or agreement because trust has broken down and been replaced by anger and resentment. A skilled mediator can help to uncover misunderstandings and expose the real issues in dispute. In this way conflict can be reduced and it may, in the end, be possible to achieve reconciliation between private individuals or business people who are in a continuing relationship.

Saving time and money Mediation will often lead to quicker settlements than would be achieved through litigation procedures and, as a result of time-saving, can reduce legal and other costs.

Reducing stress Because of its informality and potential for time-saving, mediation offers dispute resolution that is less stressful for the parties than court litigation.

THE NEED TO REDUCE STRESS

Mediation: experiments and experience

Although there is an ever-increasing interest in mediation today, some forms of it have a long history, and have been used in many parts of the world, for example to deal with employment or international disputes. 'Fighting for rights' is characteristic of Anglo-American approaches to litigation, but countries with different traditions of resolving disputes have devised less contentious methods of dealing with conflict that focus on conciliation. The use of neutrals to help disputing parties reach agreement has been common in China and Africa, and is increasingly being used in Japan.

The current interest in ADR in many parts of the world can be attributed to four principal concerns: avoiding the cost and delay of court proceedings and coping with court congestion; improving access to justice; offering more effective methods of dispute resolution; and offering the public more opportunity to participate in dispute resolution.

In the USA there has been a steady increase since the 1960s in the development of mediation for industrial disputes, small claims, family and neighbour disputes, in order to relieve court congestion. The experience there suggests that mediation can save time and legal costs in civil disputes and that mediation users generally express considerable satisfaction with the process, even when they are required to enter mediation programmes attached to courts. Results have been so positive that in 1998 the US Congress, finding that ADR using properly trained mediators provided a variety of benefits, including 'greater satisfaction of the parties, innovative methods of resolving disputes, and greater efficiency in achieving settlements', passed the Alternative Dispute Resolution Act. Under this Act all district courts now require litigants in civil cases to consider the use of an ADR process at an appropriate stage in the litigation, and each district court has a responsibility to provide litigants in all civil cases with at least one ADR process.

ADR has also become popular in Canada, Australia, South Africa and New Zealand for commercial disputes, employment disputes, family and divorce, neighbourhood disputes and disputes with government.

ADR has been used less frequently in parts of Europe where litigation is generally less expensive than in the UK or US, although the Netherlands and some Central European states have recently begun to show an interest in developing it.

In England the Advisory, Conciliation and Arbitration Service (ACAS) was established in 1972 to conciliate complaints of unfair dismissal in cases being taken to Industrial Tribunals (now Employment Tribunals). Conciliation as an Alternative Dispute Resolution process in separation and divorce has been growing steadily since its introduction in the late 1970s. More recently there has been an emphasis on the development of family mediation services, and the UK College of Family Mediators was founded in 1996 to promote and maintain standards of conduct among family mediators. In the field of commercial and other business disputes a number of organisations, such as the Centre for Dispute Resolution (CEDR) and ADR Group, have been established in the last ten years to train mediators and to carry out mediations. There has also been a recent growth in local neighbourhood mediation schemes, where volunteers help to resolve disputes between neighbours free of charge. The umbrella organisation Mediation UK covers a network of organisations and individuals that provide community mediation, mostly dealing with neighbour disputes, throughout England, Wales, Scotland, and Northern Ireland.

A number of mediation developments have taken place in Scotland and Wales. A study of ADR in Scotland in 1996 concluded that ADR services were 'embryonic', and that although family mediation was well established, there was a lack of activity within the commercial and consumer spheres. However, the research suggested that there were prospects for the expansion of mediation services within the community and neighbourhood sphere. The first Scottish community mediation project was established in Edinburgh in 1995 and is accredited by Mediation UK. There is another mediation scheme at Edinburgh Central Citizens' Advice Bureau for non-family civil disputes of any value linked to the Edinburgh Sheriff Court. This project has been funded by Citizens' Advice Scotland and has recently received funds from the European Social Fund to continue its work. The Law Society of Scotland has since July 1994 promoted an ADR service (ACCORD) and accredits solicitors trained in mediation techniques.

In North Wales a community mediation service covering Gwynedd, including Anglesey, is being set up to deal with neighbourhood conflict. Most of those involved in the service will be

Welsh speakers and all meetings have been bilingual. Mediation Mid Wales provides independent mediators who deal with neighbour disputes in Powys.

The almost limitless possibilities for mediation are illustrated by the growth of mediation schemes in novel areas. For example, the YMCA in Sussex is running a pilot mediation service for young people in dispute with their families or who are estranged from their families and want to make contact again. Battersea Citizens' Advice Bureau/Law Centre plans to offer mediation for disputes involving school exclusions. A further area of mediation development is victim/offender mediation where the mediation process is designed to help the perpetrators of criminal offences understand the impact of their behaviour on victims and allows the victims to come fact to face with the perpetrators. This process can be helpful for victims in coming to terms with what has happened to them and in the rehabilitation of offenders.

New mediation schemes for civil disputes

Because of the potential advantages of settling legal disputes through mediation, a number of special ADR schemes have been set up in London and other parts of the country, as we have seen. Several of these are attached to courts.

One of the most important developments is the Central London County Court's mediation scheme, which has been running for over two years (since May 1996) and is offered for civil disputes where the amount of money at stake is higher than the limit for the small claims track (see page 12; previously it was offered in disputes involving sums over £3,000). The CLCC mediation scheme is designed for fast- and multi-track claims where more complicated court procedures apply and in which heavy legal costs may have to be paid. It is the first of its kind and has now been placed on a permanent footing by the Lord Chancellor. A similar scheme is being run in the Bristol County Court with the co-operation of the Bristol Law Society and it seems that courts around the country are becoming interested in developing their own mediation schemes.

Since 1993, judges in the Commercial Court (part of the High Court in London) have been issuing ADR orders at an early stage in some large commercial disputes. Once an ADR order has been issued the parties are required to try using the services of a mediator to resolve their dispute before being allowed to continue with the litigation, and the court will want to know what steps they have taken to do so.

More recently the Court of Appeal has launched a pilot ADR scheme where certain types of appeal cases are mediated by senior lawyer-mediators who provide their services free of charge.

The Department of Health is also organising a mediation scheme for cases of medical negligence. Disputes where people sue doctors over poor medical treatment are often very difficult and take many years to deal with through normal court litigation. Several health authorities are co-operating in the scheme, with the aim of settling medical negligence claims at a relatively early stage in order to avoid the cost and stress of prolonged litigation.

Mediation in action

The main purpose of this book is to describe in simple terms how mediation works in action by focusing on the new mediation scheme in the Central London County Court. The mediation process is set out in Chapter 2. The experiences of disputing parties who had their cases mediated in the CLCC scheme are described in Chapter 3. Chapter 4 considers in more detail what mediation can offer to litigants in the light of the experience of the CLCC scheme. Chapter 5 explains the role solicitors can play in preparing their clients for mediation and in advising them during mediation sessions. Chapter 6 provides practical guidance on how to arrange mediation and what to consider before attending a mediation. The final chapter looks at what developments are likely in ADR as a result of government policy and the approach of judges in court.

Chapter 2

How Does Mediation Work?

When does mediation ooour?

Mediation can take place at any stage in a dispute: *before* any court proceedings have started; as soon as court proceedings have commenced; at any time *after* proceedings have commenced and before trial; it can even take place the day before a trial. In short, parties can choose to try and resolve their dispute by mediation at any stage in the dispute, although the advantages in terms of time and cost will be greater the sooner mediation is undertaken and the dispute is ended.

Who conducts mediations?

Both lawyers and non-lawyers can become mediators and a number of organisations run training courses for them. Such courses provide background for mediators on how disputes arise and obstacles to settling disputes, and training in specific mediation skills, such as communication, negotiation, breaking deadlocks in discussions, handling difficult people, settlement options.

The selected mediator may have a specialist knowledge of the subject matter of the dispute. For example, if the problem is over building works it is often helpful if the mediator is a surveyor in addition to having some knowledge of the law, so that they can make a useful contribution on the subject under dispute as well as on the legal framework.

Generally people are free to choose their own mediator from lists of accredited mediators kept by the mediation organisations (see page 60). A solicitor can arrange this, otherwise anyone handling a dispute themselves should contact a mediation organisation directly for advice and then agree with the other party who the mediator should be. If the disputing parties are not in communication, one side can still contact a mediation organisation, which may get in touch with the other side to see if they can be persuaded to try mediation. If the

Architect v. client

An architect had not received payment of his final bill for work carried out on a private flat. After asking for payment for a year and a half he finally issued court proceedings and the case was mediated. The architect, who had not consulted solicitors, accepted the court's offer of mediation because he did not feel that the money at stake (about £4,000) warranted legal fees, but on the other hand he said, 'it is not a sum of money I am prepared to let go. This has taken ages writing letters and it would take even longer if I went to court.'

The flat-owner's complaint was that the final bill had been much higher than expected, the quality of some of the work was poor and, because of lengthy building works, relations with neighbours had deteriorated. He said: 'This is a classic situation of communication breakdown. For a layman this was a very big project. Supporting walls had to be removed. There was a great deal of stress about the building project, but we went into it with our eyes open and took great care to take precautions. Our consultants and advisers were the best. We asked questions as we went along but no proper answers were given. They never apologised to us. Never once. The effect of that one single project has led to a whole lever-arch file of correspondence with our managing agents and we have been threatened with eviction by our landlord because the owners say that the building might fall down!'

During the course of the mediation an apology from the architect was read out to the flat-owner, which said: 'The plaintiff regrets any inconvenience and stress that has resulted to you and your family.' After this formal apology the parties managed to reach a settlement whereby the flat-owner paid £2,500 of the outstanding bill and both sides agreed that would be an end to the litigation. In less than three hours the parties had managed to reach an agreement ending a dispute that had been going on for almost two years. At the end the architect said: 'I think mediation is a very good idea. It just short-circuits the whole business. Although I'm not happy with the outcome, the case was not financially worth pursuing further through the court. I haven't been to business school but even I know that!'

mediation is part of a scheme operated by a court then the court may appoint an accredited mediator. More information on arranging mediation is given in Chapter 6.

What happens in mediation?

Mediation sessions can take place in rooms in a court building, in the offices of a solicitor or barrister or other professional, or even in a hotel. The length of the mediation session tends to depend on the type of dispute and whether or not it is part of a court scheme. Disputes over relatively small sums of money or where the issues are not very complicated can usually be mediated in half a day, whereas in some large commercial disputes the mediation might last for more than a day. The Central London County Court limits its mediation sessions to three hours.

It is important for the mediation session to be in comfortable surroundings and to be conducted in an atmosphere that is informal but orderly. The mediator and disputing parties (and their legal or other representatives if present) are usually seated around a table. Mediators have different ways of seating people, but arrangements are generally informal to minimise any sense of confrontation. Sometimes mediators dispense with a table and have everyone sitting in a circle.

Preliminary joint meeting

The parties are usually welcomed at a preliminary joint meeting and congratulated on having taken the step of coming to mediate their dispute. The mediator may then give a little information about him- or herself before going on to explain how the session is going

WHAT IS MEDIATION ?

to proceed, what the role of the mediator will be and what the objectives are. He or she will stress that the process is entirely voluntary and that either party is free to leave at any time if they are unhappy with the process.

Sometimes the early stages of these introductory joint meetings can be somewhat tense, especially if it is the first time that the disputing parties have been face to face, or even spoken, since the beginning of the dispute and they feel awkward or embarrassed. The mediator has to reduce tension and create a calm and constructive atmosphere. Solicitors or other representatives, if present, can help by maintaining a courteous and professional approach. Most solicitors are extremely good at this.

The opening joint session is a very important opportunity for both parties to make clear to each other the most serious aspects of their grievance and to communicate exactly what it is that they are concerned about. The mediator will usually give each about fifteen minutes to summarise, in their own words and without interruption, the nature of their complaint against the other side. People tend to find that this opportunity is a very satisfying part of the process and helpful in reaching a compromise agreement to end the dispute.

However, there are some cases where relations between the parties are so bad that they do not want to be in the same room together. If this occurs, mediatiors will carry out the mediation without any joint sessions, and merely shuttle between the parties.

Private meetings

After the opening joint session each side goes into a separate room for private meetings with the mediator (together with their legal advisers or anyone else who is accompanying them). The mediator then begins a process of 'shuttle diplomacy', exploring with each party alternately the details of their case and discussing the strengths and weaknesses of their claim. Information given to the mediator during these private sessions is strictly confidential and he or she will only pass on information to the other side if given express permission to do so. During this process the mediator tries to establish where there is common ground between the parties and to discover the scope for compromise, and will also try to identify the most important sticking points and to understand why the disputing parties take a different view of those points.

EARLY STAGES CAN BE TENSE !

Usually, after a period spent in private session the possibilities for agreement begin to emerge. The mediator will spend some time working out the exact terms of any agreement with each side to ensure that both sides are happy with them. This stage can often involve some intense bargaining, with the mediator acting as the go-between.

Concluding joint session

Once a broad agreement has been reached the mediator brings everyone back together for a final joint meeting to work out the details and to draft a document setting out the agreed terms for the disputing parties to sign. The mediator ends the mediation session by congratulating both sides on having reached a settlement and will often invite them to shake hands before they leave.

This final session can be crucially helpful in setting the tone for future relations between the parties and in laying grievances to rest. Even if the parties have not managed to reach an agreement, the mediator uses the final joint session to draw attention to the progress that has been made in clarifying the issues in dispute, and in moving closer to a settlement.

'Overall I was very pleased with the mediation. I was not confident before the mediation that the case would be settled by this method, but I'm very pleased that there was the opportunity to settle in this way.'

'There are many positive aspects to mediation. We really appreciated the highly focused approach and the businesslike manner in which the matter was conducted.'

'The atmosphere during mediation was less formal than the court room. The mediator was very fair to both sides. In conclusion I think this is an easier way of resolving simple disputes.' (Users of CLCC mediation scheme.)

CHAPTER 3

EXPERIENCES OF MEDIATION

'Mediation is quick cheap and informal. The striking feature of the whole process is the high level of consumer satisfaction. Many mediations end with the parties shaking hands and going out together. You don't often see that in our courts of law.' (His Honour Judge Neil Butter QC, who established the mediation scheme at the Central London County Court.)

'I do believe that people get themselves into disputes too easily, encouraged by solicitors and the media...What people really need is some impartial experts to explain to them the consequences of not settling their differences and the risks of going to legal process.' (User of CLCC mediation scheme.)

Mediation in the Central London County Court

The Central London County Court (in Park Crescent, W1) has run a pilot mediation scheme since 1996 – the first of its kind in this country – with the aim of providing a model for other courts to follow. It was put on a permanent footing in 1998. The scheme gives people involved in court litigation at the CLCC, whether private individuals, businesses, institutions or public bodies, the chance to have their dispute mediated by a trained mediator at a very early stage in the case, rather than following the normal often lengthy court procedures. It offers an informal way of settling disputes, *after* court proceedings have begun, that may save time and expense and some of the worry involved in a court case.

The scheme was set up with the co-operation of leading mediation organisations, which has made it possible for the CLCC to provide the service for only £25 for each party. It is entirely voluntary and people are informed of it by a leaflet sent out by the court as soon as proceedings have been started. If both disputing parties agree to try mediation then the court appoints a trained mediator and will contact each side or their solicitors to arrange a convenient date. The

27

court meanwhile suspends its usual timetable and procedures until after the mediation has taken place. If the dispute is settled at the mediation that will be the end of the case; if not, then the normal court timetable will resume, and continue to trial, unless the parties manage to settle the case before the date of the court hearing. All mediations take place in the court building from 4.30 pm, after normal court hours. During mediations court staff are on hand to deal with any queries and to collect papers at the end.

Since the beginning of the CLCC scheme about two hundred cases have been mediated, most of which (about 62 per cent) ended in a settlement at the end of the three-hour mediation appointment. Of those that did not, quite a few parties managed to settle their differences soon afterwards as a result of the mediation. In the end only a small minority of cases that tried mediation actually went on to be decided by a judge in court.

Because the CLCC scheme was unique when it was established, the Lord Chancellor's Department commissioned an intensive study of how it was working during the first two years of its operation. The study looked at the kinds of cases being mediated, the reasons for trying mediation, satisfaction with the mediation process and with the outcome of the mediations. The material in the remainder of this chapter and the following chapters is drawn from that study.

The types of cases mediated

CLCC offers its mediation service to people whose claims are valued above the small claims limit (see page 12). The people who have tried it have been involved in quite a variety of disputes and generally over fairly substantial amounts of money – between £3,000 and £10,000. In about a quarter of cases the parties were arguing about sums in excess of £15,000. Typical kinds of cases to be successfully mediated were complaints about poor workmanship, failure to pay for services received, or problems between landlords and tenants. Many of the disputes were between two businesses, while some involved private individuals suing businesses or vice versa. A small number were claims for compensation after injury in a road traffic accident. Most parties had tried to resolve the dispute before starting court proceedings but had failed, often resulting in quite a lot of bad feeling between the opposing sides.

Some cases mediated in the CLCC scheme

Complaints about shoddy workmanship

'I had had some work carried out on my shop premises. The building work was of poor quality. On completion ... it was discovered that the ceiling had not been done properly and I had to get someone to do it all over again.'

Failure to pay for services received

'We carried out some work for the other party which should have been paid for on delivery. But the payment was not made and it was three months later that a complaint was made about the quality of work that we had done.'

Poor service

'We had taken a holiday during which we had a catalogue of complaints about the poor standards of accommodation and service at the resort.'

'My luggage was lost by an airline and they would not repay the value of the luggage.'

Employment problems

'I was unfairly dismissed from work and was claiming pay and severance under the terms of my contract.'

Personal injury

'I had a terrible reaction to a cosmetic and as a result I was injured. My face was covered with a rash and this prevented me from working as usual.'

'I was claiming compensation for a broken arm suffered in a road accident.'

Landlord and tenant

'I wanted the local authority to carry out repairs to my flat.'

'I was claiming against my tenant for the cost of repairs that I had to carry out at end of his tenancy.'

Reasons for choosing mediation

Plaintiffs

'I was claiming for my salary which was owed to me by the defendant for whom I had worked previously. I tried mediation because it sounded like a cheaper and less formal way of settling the dispute as opposed to going to court.'

'I was suing the local council to get compensation for failure to do repairs to my flat. When my solicitor told me that mediation existed I decided it would be a good idea as it would probably be sorted out with both sides being content with the final outcome.'

'We wanted payment for erecting scaffolding as per the quotation and drawings. We tried mediation because to proceed to trial would have been too costly. There was a case for both sides to answer. This was in my opinion the best way to try and resolve the problem.'

Defendants

'We didn't pay the amount of money claimed by the plaintiff due to the fact that there had been a delay of six months for delivery of the equipment we ordered. We tried mediation because we thought we would have more control of the settlement of dispute by the company. We [the directors] knew the facts very well. We had no confidence in solicitors. We would have no legal fees to pay.'

'It was a dispute over architect's fees. The architect overcharged us and we would not accept the bill. We tried mediation because our company had dealt with these architects for over ten years, therefore felt it would be a "nicer" way to deal with the dispute and complete the situation.'

'We felt that we had made a reasonable offer to settle which the plaintiffs had not accepted out of pique. There did not seem to be much doubt about the law and we felt that an independent skilled negotiator would resolve the deadlock without recourse to lawyers.'

Why choose mediation?

Most people tried the CLCC mediation scheme because they hoped to settle their dispute more quickly and cheaply than by going to trial. Many worried about being involved in a long-drawn-out court action and being faced with a large bill from their solicitor at the end of the case. Some were not keen on the idea of having to give evidence at a trial and preferred the option of trying to hammer out differences in an informal setting.

Some people tried mediation because they knew the other party quite well and wanted to resolve the dispute in a way that was less confrontational than going to court – for example small businesses involved in a dispute with a supplier or professional they had worked with for some years. Another reason was to avoid having to involve solicitors, either because of a lack of confidence in them or through frustration at having to hand over the case rather than deal directly with the other side.

What do the users think of mediation?

The vast majority of people were pleased with the mediation process. They liked the informality, the relaxed atmosphere, the opportunity to talk in normal everyday language rather than in legal jargon, and the fact that discussions concentrate on the issues in the dispute and not on legal technicalities. In court the unfamiliar legal terminology can leave people feeling excluded from their own case. Mediators use ordinary language and address themselves directly to those involved in the dispute, even if they are accompanied by a solicitor. The focus is on the disputing parties, their dispute and their settlement of it, and as a result they feel fully involved in the process.

Another thing that people liked about mediation was that it provided the chance to explain fully to the other side what their complaint was, in their own words and without being interrupted. This opportunity to let off a bit of steam was often helpful in paving the way toward compromise. Too often disputes escalate because people stop communicating with each other. Telephone calls are not returned, letters go unanswered and one side becomes increasingly angry and frustrated at the impossibility of finding out exactly what is going on and why the problem cannot be solved. That is often when

Likes

'I liked the opportunity to state and hear both sides of the argument without interruption or adversarial questioning and the dispassionate, disinterested assessment of the chances of my case (were it to proceed to court) that came from the mediator.'

'I liked being in a different room from my opponents. I was very worried about seeing any of them again. If we had gone to court I would have had to see much more of them and that worried me. I thought the mediator was nice and friendly and listened to me. He stood in my room listening with his foot against the wall. I don't think judges do that. They sit in huge chairs above you, look down at you and wear wigs and gowns.'

'I liked the informality – the icebreaker between plaintiff and defendant. It was a relaxed mediation and we were allowed refreshments while mediating. The ego or legal arguments are not very important. The parties just try to sort out their differences.'

'The service is excellent. Although there will always be a "winner" we feel that the process is very good. It saves time and legal costs and this is a major issue for us. We hope this idea will become widely used.'

'I liked the mediator's ability to address the weak spots. His ability to keep moving when the plaintiff was being obnoxious. His ability to direct without it appearing too apparent.'

'I thought the mediator dealt with the matter fairly and raised issues with me that I had not considered myself which persuaded me to settle the matter at the mediation.'

people decide to involve lawyers or issue court proceedings in order to try and put pressure on the other side to deal with the issue. Unfortunately, once those steps have been taken, direct communication becomes even more difficult. Mediation can re-establish lines of communication and can also go some way to repairing relationships, by clearing up misunderstandings and helping each side to see a little of

---

Dislikes

'I felt the mediator was just trying to sort the dispute with no interest in my case or my costs as long as it was settled. At the time of the mediation my legal costs were approximately £14,000. He asked me if I would drop my claim if they dropped the counter-claim against me, even though I had spent £14,000. This said it all.'

'The mediator should be given more power to make some sort of a decision. Some cases are straightforward enough to do this out of court. Having a low-cost means of settling disputes without recourse to the courts is a good idea.'

'The mediator should be able to offer an opinion at the end of the proceedings. Particularly in a case such as mine where I believe our case was so strong. This would have benefited me – speedier resolution, and the defendant would have saved on his costs.'

---

the other's point of view. One plaintiff gave an example of this situation in a dispute over the cost of building works:

'We went for legal proceedings only reluctantly as we wished for, and far preferred the idea of a meeting to discuss the dispute and settle it with the defendant. We accepted mediation as soon as the court offered it, though the defendant initially refused it. The adversarial and more legally oriented route through the courts seemed from the first to be less likely to achieve an outcome which we would all be happy to accept.'

There was also general approval of the skills and qualities of the mediators. Most people who used the mediation service said that they had confidence in their mediator and felt that he or she was neutral and unbiased. Some business people commented on how quickly the mediator grasped and focused on the business issues involved in the case.

People were more likely to have reservations about the mediation process if their cases had not been settled and they were frustrated at the failure to reach an agreement. Causes of complaint tended to be either that they had felt under too much pressure to settle the case or that not enough pressure had been brought to bear on the other side.

Outcomes of mediation

Those who settled their cases generally took the view that the outcome of the mediation had been fair, even though almost all accepted a lower sum of money than they had originally been claiming, usually in order to end the dispute and save legal costs. Some people needed the money urgently and so were prepared to take less in order to avoid waiting for the outcome of a court hearing. Some were worried that even if they went to court, they might not win the case – or if they did that they would not be awarded more by the judge than their opponent was willing to pay at the mediation session. Often people just wanted to get on with their lives and be rid of the trouble and anxiety involved in the legal dispute.

Why people settle for less than claimed

'It was a commercial decision. We wanted to save legal costs and maintain our relationship with the defendant.'

'I was worried about the risk of losing in court. I was also sorry for the defendant who had no assets.'

'We needed the money. We were not sure that we would get more in court.'

'I was anxious to resolve the matter so I could direct my efforts to my business. In past experience legal costs have resulted in hollow victories and I did not want to incur costs and be uncertain of the outcome.'

'I was about to retire and I wanted to conclude an aggravating matter.'

'It was a question of weighing up the chances of winning the court case, what would be paid to us, what would be the costs as against a reduced settlement at mediation with minimal cost.'

Summing up

The experience of those who tried the CLCC mediation scheme suggests that, in the great majority of cases, mediation is felt to provide a quick, informal and satisfactory way of settling disputes without having to go through the cost, anxiety and delay of a full trial in court. About 62 per cent of mediations on the CLCC scheme settled at the end of the three-hour session, and another 18 per cent settled some time after the mediation. When asked whether or not they would try mediation again if faced with a similar situation, 85 per cent said they would definitely or probably use it again. A few people were so enthusiastic about the experience that they thought it should be made compulsory for disputing parties to try mediation before going on to trial.

So, although only a comparatively small number of those offered mediation in the CLCC agreed to try it, the results of the two-year pilot scheme do suggest that mediation can offer a useful alternative method of dispute resolution even after court proceedings have been started.

'It is a pity that the service was not available in earlier years. It would probably have prevented long protracted legal wrangles between both parties, reduced costs, reduced time and brought about a speedier settlement. I can foresee that as the scheme progresses it will save considerable court time and expense for everyone involved. Plus the informality should enable parties to answer questions without the intimidation of a court atmosphere and that is especially important for the layman who is not used to legal procedures and rules which can often stop the truth emerging.' (A satisfied user of the CLCC scheme.)

Tenant v. local council

A tenant was suing the local council for compensation of about £10,000 for failure to do repairs on his flat. The case had been going on for several years and his solicitor thought it should have settled much earlier.

'This has been going on for years and the plaintiff has got Legal Aid. We all agreed to mediation. It seemed a sensible move because the alternative is a three-day trial, which will be stressful and expensive. The case should settle. No offer of money has been made by the other side. We put forward a sum for them to consider. I have no idea why it is not settling.'

The council's housing officers also accepted the mediation offer because they were interested in mediation and wanted to see how it worked. 'We are interested in saving costs and time. There are only ten people in our department and we have a lot of cases. Cases can take four to five days if they go to court. The costs are very high. We just had a bill from a case that settled and the plaintiff's legal costs were £20,000. Win or lose they drag the cases out because they get their costs at the end of the day. Ninety per cent of plaintiffs have Legal Aid. On this case we think we are liable for some works, but we have a good counter-claim against the plaintiff.'

Despite the fact that the mediation took place only four weeks before the trial and when the parties were still apparently at loggerheads, they managed to reach a satisfactory agreement by the end of the three-hour mediation session. The tenant accepted £5,500 plus his legal costs. After the mediation he said that he thought the amount of money was fair and that his barrister had told him on the previous day that a fair settlement would be between £5,000 and £6,000.

The defendants were also satisfied with the settlement. 'The case has been going on a long, long time. We have avoided the costs of trial, the barrister's costs and our housing officer's time. The settlement reflects our concerns about our counter-claim. We think it is a fair outcome and we are pleased it is over and done with. The housing officer who attended the mediation commented: 'Because it is so informal here, both parties can get what they want. It makes future relations easier. I am locked into a relationship with the plaintiff.'

CHAPTER 4

WHAT CAN MEDIATION OFFER?

When people find themselves in the middle of a dispute they usually do not immediately rush off to consult a lawyer about going to court. They are more likely to try and sort out the situation by dealing directly with the other person involved. This is how the vast majority of everyday disputes are resolved. People generally only consider taking legal action when the normal ways of dealing with disputes have been unsuccessful. Seeking legal advice or beginning court proceedings are not steps that most people take lightly. They do it because the matter is important to them and because there seems to be no other way of achieving what they want.

A solicitor, once involved in a dispute, will also generally try to settle the case before recommending court action, and even then will put a lot of energy into negotiating with the other side to try and reach a settlement before going to trial. Solicitors are of course very aware of the cost of court proceedings, of the time that cases take to prepare, and of the disruption to normal life and business that that entails. They also know the risks and that no matter how strong a case appears to be there can never be 100 per cent certainty that the client will win. After all, in every court case one side ends up losing.

Why is it difficult to resolve some disputes?

Although many cases are, in the end, settled before a court hearing, this often happens at quite a late stage and after a lot of time and money have been spent by each side. Why then is it so difficult to resolve disputes at an early stage and without resorting to court action? It is hard to provide a simple explanation because all disputes are different and are influenced by many factors – including the personalities of the people involved. Solicitors who had advised their clients to try mediating their disputes in the Central London County Court's scheme explained why they thought it had not been possible to settle earlier. Common reasons were:

- that both sides were absolutely convinced of the strength of their claim or their defence
- that there had been a breakdown of communication between the parties
- that there was a lot of bad feeling between the parties
- that one side was being very unrealistic about the chances of success
- that one side was being very aggressive
- that the defendant was simply trying to delay payment.

Once people have begun legal proceedings the opportunities for direct contact are reduced. Correspondence and conversations tend to be conducted between solicitors. The disputing parties seek to protect their position and, in the absence of face-to-face communication, become angry and suspicious of each other. The result is often an increased sense of injustice and an unwillingness to compromise the claim.

The accounts given by some of the litigants in the CLCC mediation scheme as to why they had not been able to settle earlier confirm many of the reasons mentioned by the solicitors. For example, a defendant who had building works carried out on his premises was very unhappy with what had been done. He had had to bring in other contractors to redo some of the work and had therefore refused to pay the original builder's entire final bill. He was unwilling to have any discussions about the dispute with the builder – who then sued him for payment. The defendant said:

'I refused to have several meetings with him... because when we spoke on the phone and talked about this problem he did get a bit argumentative about it and I wasn't prepared to get into conflicts and direct arguments and all the rest of it and I knew that if I was going to meet him and discuss it in his office or my office then we would only finish up having an argument and just making the matter worse really. I like to do things in black and white. If you've got anything to say just put it on paper and everything's recorded and if it did go to court you've got your evidence, both sides.'

In another case a dispute arose between two businesses over the terms of a contract, despite the fact that they had been trading with each other for years. When asked why the dispute could not have been sorted out amicably without mediation the defendant said that

Solicitors' views on why cases hadn't been settled before mediation

'Neither side was prepared to accept they had both made mistakes. The defendant would not pay a small outstanding invoice. My client issued proceedings without seeking legal advice. When a counter-claim was made he took advice, but by then both parties had taken entrenched positions.'

'The parties were at odds as to the issues in the dispute and their respective positions as to the amount of compensation were vastly different. These views changed during mediation resulting in settlement.'

'The solicitors were corresponding about legal issues only. No one was addressing the relationship involved between the plaintiff and the defendant.'

'The parties had not had the opportunity to sit down together to try and resolve problems between them.'

'The parties focused on the perceived rights and wrongs of the other side's actions rather than on the commercial realities of the case. Communication between the parties was also slow.'

'The plaintiff was representing herself and was therefore determined not to settle for less than her claim. We wanted a more rapid resolution and an opportunity to put a reasonable offer to her. She briefly sought legal advice, but her solicitor consistently failed to respond to letters or telephone calls offering settlement.'

'Both parties believed genuinely that they were right.'

'The defendant's solicitors are renowned for taking an aggressive line and were constantly pursuing us with aggressive tactics.'

'The costs implications of a full trial were not looming quite so largely earlier on.'

he had been surprised to find himself embroiled in litigation.

'It was one of those things that really should never have gone to court. We should have been able to sort this out. We had had a long relationship and I had one meeting with the plaintiff and after that meeting I sent him a letter which was probably a pretty firm expression of what we were going to do as we understood the agreement and that included not paying them until they performed, but that's as far as our discussions went. The next thing we knew we got the writ.'

How can mediation help?

Although mediation will never provide the answer to all cases, it can help to resolve disputes where there is scope for compromise but where normal negotiations, with or without solicitors, have failed. If each side agrees to try mediation, that suggests they are not hell-bent on going to court and are at least willing to try to reach an agreement that will end the litigation.

Getting people face to face

The mediation session is often the first time that disputing parties will have spoken directly to each other for a long time. Just physically being around a table and having the chance to talk about the dispute is very important and something that rarely happens in normal settlement negotiations involving lawyers. Solicitors tend to conduct negotiations by telephone or letter, and offers, rejections, and counter-offers are all made through them. This can be a lengthy process and it is unlikely that at any point the parties will come together with their advisers to discuss offers face to face. The statement by the following defendant, who had refused to make any offers of settlement before mediation, illustrates the value of bringing people together:

'The whole idea of me going to court in the first place was because I felt I had a very strong case and I don't think he would have got anything... Basically I wasn't prepared to pay anything. It was as simple as that. I wouldn't have been under normal circumstances prepared to pay anything. It was only actually coming along to the mediation, I thought, "Oh well. He's not a bad guy. Maybe let's see if we can just maybe soften a little bit and come to some sort of compromise."'

Identifying the issues

As disputes escalate, the real issues that people care about can sometimes become obscured. Discussing the case around a table helps to identify the crucial matters that have to be resolved, which points the parties agree on, and where they definitely disagree. Even if a mediation is not successful, it can be very helpful in pinning down the issues that the parties and their lawyers will have to concentrate on if a settlement is to be achieved at a later date.

Probing the case

The mediator can probe the basis of the claim and the defence in private discussions with each side, playing devil's advocate from a position of neutrality. Once the parties have talked over the issues with the mediator, and discussed the other side's perspective on their claims, they may see their case in a different light and may alter their view of the strength of their position.

Letting people agree their own settlements

When communication is re-established through mediation and the mediator talks to the parties in private about the scope for achieving a settlement, each can reveal, in confidence, what kind of agreement they would be happy with. Once people are being frank about what they want, rather than adopting negotiating stances, it can become clear that the distance between what each side wants is actually much smaller than has been apparent previously.

In court the possible outcome is generally winning or losing a sum of money. Mediation can allow a more creative agreement to emerge that both sides will find acceptable and that will help to keep the relationship intact for the future, if that is what is wanted. People can work out their own terms and come to whatever arrangement suits them and is most likely to provide a permanent resolution to the problem. Skilled mediators can be very helpful in sensing the potential for interesting settlements and in suggesting creative alternatives.

Resolving disputes and reducing conflict

Parties to litigation rarely shake hands at the end of a hearing – rather, the losing party goes away to lick his or her wounds and sometimes even the winning party may feel unsatisfied with the judgement and cheated of any kind of apology from the loser. A previously good relationship between the parties prior to the dispute is unlikely to be rebuilt on the basis of a court hearing. Moreover, a defendant ordered to pay a sum of money may default on payment, thus leading to the necessity of the plaintiff beginning litigation again to get the court to force them to pay up.

Because the mediation process is directed toward defusing conflict and maximising the scope for compromise, a successful mediation has a greater potential than court adjudication for bringing a dispute finally to an end and for removing some of the bad feeling that has inevitably arisen. Moreover, an express apology can be a part of the agreement.

In one mediation that took place in the CLCC scheme the parties were brought back together in the middle of the mediation process so that the defendant could say personally how sorry he was that accusations that appeared to be untrue had been made against the plaintiff. This was done because the plaintiff had felt so badly wronged that he could not begin to consider the possibility of settling the dispute until the apology had been forthcoming. For his part, the defendant had not realised how strongly the plaintiff felt about this matter, or how genuinely offended the plaintiff had been. The defendant made a sincere statement of apology directly to the plaintiff in front of the mediator, after which the mediation proceeded fairly rapidly toward settlement. At the end of the mediation the plaintiff and defendant were able to shake hands before they left.

In another case that had been going on for a very long time the plaintiff said that the receipt of an apology provided the greatest satisfaction of all. 'The mediator made the defendant apologise for the way he had treated me. That was the best part.'

Of course in many cases the disputing parties are not in a continuing relationship and they may not care whether they receive an apology or not. What they want is a sum of money and for the case to be over with. In such situations a successful mediation offers the chance of achieving these objectives through an informal, non-confrontational process that can reduce rather than increase conflict and stress and that may lead to a more certain end to the dispute by increasing the chances that the agreement will be honoured.

CHAPTER 5

THE ROLE OF LAWYERS
IN MEDIATION

It is perfectly possible to arrange mediation without the help of a
solicitor, and this will be covered in the next chapter. However, very
many people who become entangled in a legal dispute do go to a
lawyer for advice and this chapter is aimed at those people and their
solicitors. So what part can lawyers play in advising about mediation,
in preparing their clients to attend mediation alone, or in
accompanying and advising them during the sessions?

Giving advice about mediation

The growth of mediation as an alternative method of resolving civil
disputes is a relatively new development in England, so many lawyers
are still not entirely familiar with how it works in practice and only a
small minority have had experience of mediation sessions. It may not
therefore occur to them to suggest it to a client as an option.
However, in giving the best advice about how to deal with disputes,
solicitors should consider whether mediation might be a useful
alternative approach: for example when the usual attempts to reach a
settlement through ordinary negotiations have failed; when they are
considering issuing court proceedings; or when proceedings have
been started *against* their client. Even when it seems likely that the
client will eventually reach an agreement with their opponent,
mediation may speed up the process, bringing the case to a more rapid
conclusion and thus saving the client time and possibly legal costs.

Which kinds of cases?

Mediation organisations suggest that mediation can be used in most
kinds of legal disputes and the results of the scheme in the Central
London County Court show that it can be successful in a very wide
range of cases.

Mediation seems to be particularly appropriate where the likely
costs of a legal case will be out of proportion to the amount of money
that is being disputed and where the parties are keen to achieve a quick

settlement of the case. It is an attractive option when parties are private individuals who will be personally responsible for the legal costs; where small businesses want to minimise the time and costs involved in pursuing or defending a legal case; and where the opponent in the case

---

Why solicitors advise mediation

'The client wanted a quick result. He has been involved in litigation before and knows about delay. It was a simple claim. If it had gone to trial the costs would have been far in excess of the claim itself if the client had lost.'

'I felt it was an appropriate case for mediation. It was a straightforward road traffic accident. There were disputes on both liability and quantum [the amount of compensation to be paid] and I felt it would achieve a quicker settlement than waiting for a trial date.'

'The size of the claim was less than £10,000. The attitude of my client (the defendant) was receptive. The plaintiff was a litigant in person. We felt that we had a good case but the unrepresented plaintiff had taken criticism of his services very personally and would not listen to reason. The amount he ultimately settled for was no more than we had already offered. However the mediation gave him his day in court and meant that he had no axe to grind against the mediator.'

'My client was short of funds and also keen to put the case behind him for psychological reasons. We thought that mediation would mean the case settled sooner.'

'The case was expected to settle. Mediation was likely to speed up the process and enable both sides to see potential weaknesses as viewed by an independent person.

'It was mainly the cost considerations. We felt we had a good case but going to trial for less than £40,000 is extravagant and the defendants had made no settlement offers. This was a way of settling but without either side losing face.'

---

is not being advised by a solicitor and so may have a rather unrealistic approach to the strengths and weaknesses of their claim in law. Solicitors who advised their clients to try the mediation service at the CLCC were often influenced by these kinds of considerations.

When to mediate?

It is also clear from the cases mediated in the CLCC scheme that mediation can take place *at any point* in the life of a case. Although, as we have seen, the earlier the mediation occurs the greater any time and cost savings are likely to be, mediation can produce satisfactory settlements even when cases have been going on for a very long time and the mediation takes place shortly before the trial, as the following example from the CLCC scheme illustrates.

In a long-running partnership dispute over a business the parties disagreed about the accounts and how the proceeds of the sale of the business should be divided. The dispute had been going on for over three years and had not settled, in the view of the defendant's solicitor, because the plaintiff had greatly overestimated the amount that he was likely to receive in the division of money.

Even though a trial date had been set the solicitor recommended mediation because 'the costs of the impending trial of the action were likely to be more than my clients could afford'. The plaintiff agreed to try mediation and the case settled at the end of the three-hour mediation session. As the defendant's solicitor commented, 'both sides were obliged to recognise that each had points of view that had to be respected'.

Preparing clients for attending mediation sessions alone

In quite a few cases in the CLCC mediation scheme, clients came to the mediation session without their solicitor – perhaps because they did not feel the need for assistance or because they wanted to keep down costs – and this generally worked perfectly well. There are, however, certain steps that solicitors can usefully take to prepare their clients. For example, they can explain what will happen at the mediation session; advise them about what they need to consider before they go and what they should take with them; and discuss what they should bear in mind when reaching an agreement to settle the dispute with the other side at the end of a mediation session.

The facts of the case

First of all, solicitors should advise clients that the mediator will want to go over the facts of the dispute. So if the case is complicated or has been going on for a long time, clients should remind themselves of the important facts and which issues they want to concentrate on. They may also find it helpful to make notes on the key points they want to cover in the opening session when they are likely to be asked to make a statement of their main grievances. Although mediations are very informal, memories can sometimes fail when people are feeling on edge in an unfamiliar situation.

Key letters or documents

Second, solicitors should consider whether it would be helpful for the client to take copies of key letters or documents with them. Although, unlike at trials, documents are not referred to a great deal during mediation sessions, having copies of important letters or other material to hand which establish whether someone did or did not say or do something at a certain time can help to back up a claim.

Contact during mediation

Third, solicitors who have been advising on a dispute should try to make arrangements so that their client can check back with them by telephone during the course of the mediation if they need to. Parties often want to finalise a settlement agreement at the end of the mediation session before everyone goes home and may want to check the main points with their solicitors first before signing the settlement document.

Agreements about costs

Finally, quite often in civil cases the question of who is to pay the costs of the action will be as important as the main terms of the agreement. Clients who go to mediations alone need to be clear about what arrangement they want to make about the payment of any legal costs if a settlement is reached. It will save time and confusion at the mediation session if solicitors have discussed this with their client in advance.

Accompanying clients at mediation sessions

Mediators like to deal directly with the disputing parties and keep them centre stage during mediation sessions, but solicitors can play an important part by offering support and advice to their clients and by helping to maintain a courteous and co-operative atmosphere. They are also often crucial in helping to draft the written agreement if a settlement is reached.

Solicitors, and sometimes barristers, accompanied their clients at most of the mediation sessions in the CLCC scheme. They had generally had no previous experience of mediation, and found that what was required of them during the session was very different from what would be expected during a court hearing. They also found that the preparation needed was much more like the preparation that would be necessary for a face-to-face settlement discussion between solicitors than that for a trial. For example, they focused on the main issues and on the strengths and weaknesses of the case, and also talked through with their clients what sort of settlement they were hoping to achieve, rather than spending time assembling evidence, rehearsing legal points or preparing for adversarial confrontation.

Lawyer-advisers are not invited to make presentations or statements during mediation except when their client prefers them to do the talking. Their contribution is in providing advice as the

---

Solicitors' preparations for mediation sessions

'The preparation was exactly the same as for a settlement meeting [between solicitors trying to negotiate an agreement prior to trial] but nothing like preparation for trial involving bundles of documents, subpoenas to witnesses, experts' reports etc.'

'I prepared a note of the main issues and relevant documents. I did not have to consider evidence or what matters needed to be considered under cross-examination. I tried to focus on the strengths and weaknesses of each side's case.'

'My preparation focused on discussions with the client as to the levels of settlement that would be acceptable, rather than on a question of evidence and preparation for the trial.'

---

discussions develop, acting as a sounding board during private sessions, and talking through the pros and cons of various settlement options.

In a few instances in the CLCC scheme lawyers did make opening statements for their clients – if for example the client had not attended personally or simply preferred them to do so – and found that they had to adapt to the informal and non-confrontational ambience of the mediation session. Rather than delivering formal arguments, they tried to give a succinct account of their client's point of view on the dispute and to stress any key issues. Some solicitors came with voluminous paperwork, but most just brought their file and had crucial documents ready to hand, even though these might not, in the event, be used.

What do solicitors think of the mediation process?

Almost all solicitors who attended a CLCC mediation session with their clients were enthusiastic about the process, despite the fact that it was generally a totally new experience for them and that most had been rather unsure about what to expect. They liked the speed and informality of mediation and felt that it could save clients legal costs. They thought that mediation provided an important opportunity for their clients to discuss their grievances directly with the other side, and that the chance to focus on the real issues of concern had paved the way for a settlement of the dispute.

They also felt that the mediators' contribution was an important aspect in reaching settlement. To achieve an agreement in a short space of time mediators need to be able to gain the confidence and respect of the disputing parties and their solicitors. They should therefore have good personal skills and be experienced and knowledgeable about the law, as well as having an understanding of the facts involved in the particular case being mediated.

'My client and I both found the mediation very helpful. The mediator was a complete professional and very fair, yet he did not get bogged down in the complexities of the contractual relationship in the way many District Judges are apt to do, especially if faced with a litigant in person. I would certainly recommend use of the procedure again if the circumstances were appropriate.'

Solicitors' views of the best aspects of mediation

'It was a relatively speedy process with an informal and relaxed atmosphere. The parties understand better what is going on. It is a chance for them to participate and really get their say, which my client found very satisfying. I hope to see it continue in a wider area. I hope to see Legal Aid being granted for this purpose in future. Potentially it could save a substantial amount of money for private clients with limited resources.'

'The best aspect is the fact that each party gets a chance to air their grievances. This means that even if the settlement is not wholly favourable it is still acceptable to the client as they feel they have had the chance to speak their mind and let the other side know how they feel.'

'It focuses the mind of the unwilling party in assessing the merits/deficiencies of their case. It reminds the confident party of the risks of litigation and in both cases it provides an independent and objective view of the strengths and weaknesses of the case directly to the parties.'

'The clients feel involved in the negotiation process and are happier with the settlements achieved.'

'Mediation takes account of personalities and their involvement in perpetuating disputes. It provides an appreciation of the fact that just because one party has a case at law it does not necessarily mean it is fair. The input of a truly neutral third party was invaluable.'

'The mediator at our particular mediation was obviously very skilled at negotiation. He managed to win the confidence of both parties and this was a major factor which led to settlement.'

Some solicitors did have criticisms of the mediation process, usually to do with the skills of the mediator – for example that they were too slow, or that they had put too much pressure on the client to settle. The fact that mediators were criticised both for being too weak and too tough indicates the importance of their being alive to the differing needs and expectations of disputing parties. There was also concern that if the mediation was not successful and the litigation continued, the mediation would actually increase the costs of the case.

Solicitors' criticisms of mediation

'I found the approach of the mediator slow, cumbersome and unduly legalistic. I felt the mediator failed to take control over the timetable of the discussions. The concluding of the settlement agreement was done in an unseemly rush. The client felt bullied into accepting a deal – it certainly didn't have a win/win feel about it.'

'The mediator concerned was unduly anxious to achieve a settlement and was prepared to adopt a bullying approach with the parties to achieve that end.'

'The mediator was not forthright enough. My client believed it could have settled that day if the mediator had been tougher.'

CHAPTER 6

ARRANGING MEDIATION

Why mediate?

You might want to try mediation for the following reasons: if you are involved in a dispute and are considering taking legal action; if the dispute is troubling you and you are having difficulty settling it by negotiation with the other side, with or without a solicitor; if you are already in the middle of legal proceedings but would like to try to settle the case rather than go to court; if the costs of proceeding with a legal case are likely to be out of proportion to the amount of money at stake; or if the case cannot be dealt with through the small claims procedure in the county court (which covers personal injury and housing claims with a value up to £1,000 and other claims with a value up to £5,000 (see page 12).

MEDIATION CAN HELP TO REMOVE BAD FEELING

When to mediate

The earlier you use mediation to settle a dispute, the greater the benefit is likely to be in saving time, cost and stress. However, mediation can take place at any time and there are many examples of cases being settled by mediation when the parties have been in conflict for years and are about to go into court. Cases have even been successfully mediated after one side has won in court and the other has launched an appeal. So it is almost never too early or too late to attempt mediation – although it is important that both sides are ready to consider settlement.

Do you need a lawyer to advise?

It is up to you to decide whether or not you want to seek legal advice before trying mediation and, if you do, whether you want your legal adviser to accompany you to the mediation. Many people do, in fact, attend mediations without a lawyer. However, it is important to remember that in most types of mediation the mediator will not be prepared to offer you legal advice. The mediator's role is to assist the parties in coming to an agreement, not to provide a ruling or to speculate about which side is likely to win in court.

If you do not seek legal advice or take a solicitor to the mediation you may possibly feel at some disadvantage. Even in cases where the facts and legal issues appear to be fairly straightforward, it may still be helpful to check the legal position first with an advice agency or a solicitor. In a complicated dispute, a solicitor is likely to be valuable in ensuring that any agreement reached is a fair reflection of the respective legal positions, and one that you will feel happy with afterwards.

It is also worth checking to see whether your opponent is likely to have legal representation at the mediation session. You may be happy to meet at a mediation on equal terms but feel relatively handicapped if your opponent appears with a legal adviser. Of course, since mediation is always a voluntary process, you do have the right to terminate the mediation if you feel at a disadvantage or if you feel unhappy about continuing with the session for any other reason. Mediators also have the power to stop a mediation if they think that the process is blatantly unfair to one side. However, it is not the mediator's job to evaluate the fairness of agreements and once a settlement has been reached and the agreement signed at the end of the mediation, both sides are bound by it. It is therefore important, if you go to a mediation without a legal adviser, that you have thought things through first. It might also be helpful to take a friend or colleague to use as a sounding board during the private sessions.

Most of the leading mediation organisations have helpful brochures about mediation, which provide checklists of matters to consider before attending a mediation session and useful hints on how to prepare.

How to choose a mediator

Mediation is still relatively new in this country and the Government does not yet regulate mediators, so it is important to be sure that the mediator you choose is properly trained and bound by codes of conduct. The Law Society has provided new codes of conduct for solicitor-mediators and all of the leading mediation organisations have their own codes of conduct for their members. A good way of finding a mediator is to contact one of the mediation organisations listed at the end of this book. They maintain lists of trained and accredited mediators and will provide help in making a choice or they will choose an appropriate mediator for you once you have told them about the details of your dispute. They may also liaise with the other side in the dispute for you over the choice of mediator.

You might want to discuss with the mediation organisation whether or not you would like your mediator to be a lawyer, or whether you want them to have expertise in a particular area. It is important to talk these matters through so that the organisation can help you make the best choice of mediator for your particular dispute.

What does it cost?

This is a difficult question to answer. In some mediation schemes the mediator makes a token charge or no charge at all. This is the situation in the Central London County Court mediation scheme (where there is a charge of £25 per party), and in the Court of Appeal ADR scheme. Many local neighbourhood mediation schemes are also free, being run by charitable organisations with the use of volunteers.

Some family mediation organisations in the 'not for profit sector' make special arrangements for couples who cannot afford to pay.

On the other hand, a number of mediation organisations provide trained mediators on a commercial basis. The rates charged tend to depend on the amount of money involved in the dispute or the complexity of the case and on how long the mediation is likely to take. In some cases there is an hourly fee, in others a flat rate, for example £700 for a day's mediation (shared between the two parties). Charges vary, so it is important to check with the various mediation organisations and compare the services and rates offered, and find out whether any administrative charge is made for arranging the mediation.

How is mediation arranged?

Through court schemes

In some mediation schemes run by courts – such as the CLCC and Court of Appeal schemes – the court undertakes all of the work involved in arranging the mediation and liaising between both sides in the dispute. Once both sides have accepted the mediation offer the court will arrange for an appropriate mediator to make contact, to organise a convenient date and time for the mediation.

Through a mediation organisation

Most trained mediators belong to one of the mediation organisations. These organisations have lists of mediators located throughout the country, and will provide information about their mediation services and offer advice about the most appropriate kind of mediator for your dispute.

Generally, when you contact one of the organisations they will discuss the case with you and advise, in confidence, whether mediation is appropriate. They will contact the other party to confirm that they are willing to mediate. The organisation will then help you to select a mediator who is acceptable to both sides and arrange a convenient date and time for the mediation. Once the mediator has been agreed, he or she will probably get in touch with both of you to answer any questions and check that everyone is prepared for the mediation. Descriptions of the activities of some of the main mediation organisations, and their contact details, are given on page 60.

55

Information about local mediation schemes can be obtained from advice agencies such as the Citizens' Advice Bureaux, the National Consumer Council and the Advice Services Alliance. The Advice Services Alliance is producing a guidance manual for advice agencies covering current ADR services. Contact details for a selection of advice agencies in England, Wales and Scotland are given on page 67. The new Community Legal Service, currently being established by the Government, will have a responsibility for providing advice about appropriate methods of resolution for civil disputes.

CHAPTER 7

THE FUTURE OF MEDIATION

'The civil justice system is there to help people resolve their disputes fairly and peacefully.' Lord Irvine, The Lord Chancellor, Modernising Justice

Lord Woolf's recommendations

Interest in the potential of mediation in civil disputes has been developing in the UK since the early 1990s; a significant step forward, however, occurred in 1996. In that year Lord Woolf MR, who is now Head of the Court of Appeal (Civil Division) published the results of a radical two-year review of the civil courts. His report contained wide-ranging proposals for changes to the procedures of the courts in order to reduce the cost, complexity, and delay in bringing civil disputes to court. He also emphasised the role of Alternative Dispute Resolution in promoting early settlement of disputes and the part that he felt the judiciary could play in encouraging people to try it.

Lord Woolf recommended that all civil courts should provide information about ADR and that Legal Aid should be made available in cases resolved by ADR before going to trial. Further, he said that court staff and the judiciary should be aware of the existing forms of ADR and should encourage their use. Perhaps more importantly for future litigants and their legal advisers, Lord Woolf also recommended that at case management conferences and pre-trial reviews parties should be required to state whether the question of ADR has been discussed and, if not, why not. Moreover, Lord Woolf suggested that in deciding on the future conduct of a case, a judge should be able to take into account the litigant's unreasonable refusal to attempt ADR. These recommendations send a clear signal that the potential of ADR for resolving civil disputes is to be taken seriously by the courts and litigating parties.

The Civil Justice Council, established as a result of Lord Woolf's Report to review the implementation of the new reforms, agreed that

ADR should be one of its main areas of work during its first year of operation and established a subcommittee on ADR to advise the Council and make recommendations.

To help educate the judiciary about the potential of mediation and other forms of ADR, the Judicial Studies Board, which is responsible for the training of the judiciary, has carried out a series of seminars for the judiciary providing information about mediation and including discussion of videos of mock mediations.

Lord Woolf's reforms of the civil courts, introduced in April 1999, give judges the power to suspend court proceedings for a limited period so that the parties to disputes can attempt to settle their case by mediation. The courts cannot force people to use mediation, but can certainly apply pressure on the parties to consider mediation seriously and to take steps towards trying to arrange it. This important new power must be viewed seriously by the courts, the litigants and the legal profession. Although judges are likely to use the power somewhat cautiously at first – where they feel that cases are clearly appropriate for mediation – it is possible that before too long we will see cases regularly directed to attempt mediation.

The Government's proposals

'People do not have to go to court if there are better ways to solve their problems.' Lord Irvine, The Lord Chancellor, *Modernising Justice*

The Government outlined plans for reforming Legal Aid, legal services and the courts in England and Wales in a White Paper, *Modernising Justice,* published in December 1998. (Scotland has a different judicial system, similar reforms have not been instituted there.) The White Paper clearly indicates the Government's interest in exploring alternatives to the courts for resolving disputes when it states that the Civil Legal Aid system 'is too heavily biased towards expensive court-based solutions to people's problems'.

Mediation and Legal Aid expenditure

According to Government figures, spending on Civil and Family Legal Aid has risen from £586 million in 1992–3 to £783 million in 1997–8. The growth in expenditure over that period is 35 per cent as compared with a general inflation figure of only 13 per cent. At the same time the number of people being helped under the Legal Aid system has actually dropped. So the increase in expenditure is accounted for by more being paid on each individual case. In the Government's view this growth in expenditure cannot continue. A range of measures are being introduced by the Government to try and stop the trend of increasing expenditure and to target Legal Aid on those cases regarded as having a high priority for public support. These measures include the establishment of a Community Legal Service Fund to replace Legal Aid; the use of block contracts with firms of solicitors providing legal services through the Community Legal Service Fund; and the encouragement of the use of 'no win no fee' arrangements with solicitors to replace Legal Aid funding for many civil cases.

An important development that reflects the Lord Chancellor's support for mediation in civil and family cases and the belief that it might be able to help in using the Legal Aid resources more efficiently, is the announcement in 1998 by the Legal Aid Board that Legal Aid funding should be extended to cover the cost of mediation for civil disputes. Moreover, it is likely that the new Legal Services Commission, which is taking over from the Legal Aid Board to administer the Community Legal Service Fund, may soon require parties who have the benefit of Legal Aid to attempt to settle their dispute by mediation *before* funding will be provided for legal representation at a court hearing.

Support for Alternative Dispute Resolution

In the White Paper the Lord Chancellor, Lord Irvine, indicated that the Government is seeking to improve the range of options available to people for resolving disputes without a formal court adjudication process. He said that ADR, including mediation, arbitration and ombudsman schemes, can be less formal and adversarial than courts, and that in some cases it may allow disputes to be resolved more quickly and cheaply. The Lord Chancellor also confirmed in a speech in November 1998 that 'the judiciary will have a significant part to play in breaking down the preconception that only a full-blown court hearing can really right a wrong'.

It seems that not only is mediation here to stay, but that the courts are likely to have an increasing role in the future in encouraging people to consider settling their differences outside of the courtroom.

Mediation Organisations

It is difficult to give clear guidance on the likely cost of mediation since this will depend on who is conducting the mediation, the type of dispute being mediated, whether the mediation is part of a special scheme, and whether the mediation organisation approached operates on a commercial or not-for-profit basis. All mediation organisations are prepared to discuss possible charges for mediation. Some of the commercial mediation organisations have a scale of fees for mediators depending on the amount of money involved in the dispute. They may also make a charge for administration. The not-for-profit family mediation organisations will set a fee for mediation sessions, but these charges may be reduced or waived depending on the financial circumstances of the mediating parties. Generally, community and neighbourhood mediation schemes are run by volunteers and the services of mediators are provided free of charge.

Some of the main mediation organisations are as follows:

1. Civil disputes (non-family)

Academy of Experts

This organisation aims to promote cost effective and efficient dispute resolution using experts. It was the first body in the UK to establish a Register of Qualified Mediators. All mediators on the Register are qualified in a professional field of expertise and in addition possess the necessary character and experience to conduct successful mediations. The Academy appoints suitably qualified mediators on request; provides the names of suitably qualified mediators for selection by disputants; and trains suitably qualified experts in the techniques of mediation. Mediators are provided for a wide range of disputes including business disputes, landlord and tenant disputes, neighbour disputes, employer and employee disputes, and personal injury cases.

Contact details:

Academy of Experts, 2 South Square, Gray's Inn, London WC1R 5HP
Tel: 0171 637 0333, Fax: 0171 637 1893, E-mail: aradatlas.co.uk

ADR Group

This private dispute resolution service was founded in 1989 by a group of lawyers, businessmen and professional mediators. The Group has a pool of trained lawyer-mediators drawn from firms of solicitors nationwide who conform to the solicitors' Code of Conduct. The Group will take on cases referred by organisations or individuals. ADR Group claims a 94 per cent settlement rate for mediated cases. It also provides training courses in negotiation and mediation. The organisation has experience in mediating a wide range of disputes on a commercial basis.

Contact details:

ADR Group, 36–38 Baldwin Street, Bristol BS1 1NR
Tel: 0117 946 7180, Fax: 0117 946 7181, Freephone 0800 61 61 30
E-mail: info@adrgroup.co.uk

Centre for Dispute Resolution (CEDR)

CEDR is an international organisation providing ADR, dispute management and conflict prevention services. It was launched in 1990 with the backing of the CBI. CEDR provides advice to parties on how ADR can help and whether it is appropriate for the case. CEDR has a team of in-house mediators and 350 accredited CEDR mediators who have successfully completed the CEDR training programme and have experience of acting as mediators. These include both lawyers and other professionals. CEDR will assist in selecting an appropriate mediator, arrange a convenient date, time and location for the mediation and then contact parties to confirm the timetable. The mediator is also likely to contact the parties before the mediation date to answer any questions and to check that he or she has relevant papers. CEDR claims a success rate of around 90 per cent. The organisation provides mediators for a wide range of disputes and has particular expertise in commercial disputes.

Contact details:
CEDR, Princes House, 95 Gresham Street, London EC2V 7NA
Tel: 0171 600 0500, Fax: 0171 600 0501
E-mail: mediate@cedr.co.uk

Chartered Institute of Arbitrators

The Institute was founded in 1915 with the aim of promoting alternative means of dispute resolution to litigation. It provides training and education for arbitrators. In addition, it maintains a list of those of its members who are prepared to offer a mediation service, which it provides on request, thereby enabling parties to approach mediators personally. In addition, the Institute has a set of rules which can be utilised alone or in conjunction with arbitration rules, if the mediation is unsuccessful.

Contact details:
Chartered Institute of Arbitrators
24 Angel Gate, City Road, London EC1V 2RS
Tel: 0171 837 4483, Fax: 0171 837 4185
E-mail: 71411.2735@compuserve.com
Website: http://www.arbitrators.org

City Disputes Panel

This organisation aims to provide a financial dispute resolution service and works for the benefit of the financial community and its clients. It offers a range of dispute resolution services including arbitration, conciliation and mediation. It also offers case evaluation and expert determination.

Contact details:
City Disputes Panel, Fifth Floor, 3 London Wall Buildings,
London EC2M 5PD
Tel: 0171 638 4775, Fax: 0171 638 4776, E-mail: CDPlondon@aol.com

Mediation UK

Mediation UK is a network of projects, organisations and individuals interested in mediation and other forms of constructive conflict resolution. It is a registered charity supported by grants and donations. The organisation has produced a Training Manual in Community Mediation Skills, a Training Course, an Accreditation Pack and a Directory. The current membership is 489 of which 178 are organisations and 311 are individuals. There are approximately 3,000 volunteers connected with the work of Mediation UK. The services offered include community/neighbourhood mediation (e.g. noisy neighbours, dogs, boundaries, children, rubbish, harassment, abuse); victim/offender mediation; and mediation/conflict resolution work in schools. The mediators do not have legal qualifications and the service is provided free of charge.

Contact details:
Mediation UK, Alexander House, Telephone Avenue, Bristol BS1 4BS
Tel: 0117 904 6661, Fax: 0117 904 3331
E-mail: mediationuk@mediationuk.org.uk

WALES

Cardiff Mediation

Friends Meeting House, 43 Charles Street, Cardiff CF1 4EB
Tel: 01222 316800, Fax: 01222 316801
E-mail: cardiff@mediation.freeserve.co

Mediation Mid Wales

Sefton House, Middleton Street, Llandrindod Wells, Powys LD1 5DG
Tel: 01597 825123

Monmouth Mediation

96 Monnow Street, Monmouth NP5 3EQ
Tel: 01600 712666

Tawe Afan Nedd Mediation

20 Craddock Street, Swansea SA1 3HE
Tel: 01792 648916, Fax: 01792 648916

SCOTLAND

Edinburgh Community Mediation Project

Free independent mediation service to assist in the resolution of community/neighbourhood disputes, e.g. noise, behaviour of children, boundary disputes, anti-social and abusive behaviour.
Contact details:
Edinburgh Community Mediation Project
27 York Place, Edinburgh EH1 3HP
Tel: 0131 557 2101, Fax: 0131 557 2102

Edinburgh Sheriff Court Advice Project/Mediation

Edinbrugh Central CAB, 58 Dundas Street, Edinburgh EH3 6QZ
Tel: 0131 557 0948, Fax: 0131 557 3543

NORTHERN IRELAND

The Mediation Network for Northern Ireland

Seeks to promote a culture of third-party intervention in conflict. Encourages individuals and agencies to improve strategies for dealing with conflict. Mediation is used to assist public bodies and institutions. Trains mediators and directly mediates in communal conflict.
Contact details:
The Mediation Network for Northern Ireland
128a Great Victoria Street, Belfast BT2 7BG
Tel: 01232 438614, Fax: 01232 314430
E-mail: info@mediation-network.org.uk
Website http://www.mediation-network.org.uk

2. Family disputes

UK College of Family Mediators

The College was founded in 1996. It sets, promotes and maintains standards of professional conduct and training for those practising family mediation. Family mediators are trained and come from a wide variety of relevant backgrounds.

Contact details:
UK College of Family Mediators,
24–32 Stephenson Way, London NW1 2HX
Tel: 0171 391 9162, Fax: 0171 391 9165
E-mail: liz.walsh@btinternet.com

A number of organisations approved by the UK College provide family mediation and related services:

Family Mediators Association (FMA)

Offers mediation on issues relating to property, finance and children following divorce or separation. Trains and supports mediators from counselling and legal backgrounds, to work in pairs or singly.

Contact details:
FMA, 46 Grosvenor Gardens, London SW1W 0EB
Tel: 0171 881 9400, Fax: 0171 881 9401
E-mail: hmcc@globalnet.co.uk

Family Mediation Scotland (FMS)

Offers mediation on children's issues relating to residence, contact and any other issues concerning children. In some locations the organisation also provides mediation for issues relating to property and finance.

Contact details:
FMS, 127 Rose Street South Lane, Edinburgh EH2 4BB
Tel: 0131 220 1610, Fax: 0131 220 6895

LawWise

Provides mediation training and consultancy for family lawyers together with administrative and developmental support for its trained mediators.

Contact details:
LawWise, The Shooting Lodge, Guildford Road, Sutton Green,

Guildford GU4 7P2
Tel: 01483 237300, Fax: 01483 237004
E-mail: a.logan@cableon.co.uk

National Family Mediation (NFM)

Offers mediation on issues relating to property and finance as well as
to children including problems of residence and contact. Mediators
come from a variety of backgrounds and often work in pairs. Also
provides training and continuing professional development for
mediators.
Contact details:
NFM, 9 Tavistock Place, London WC1H 9SN
Tel: 0171 383 5993, Fax: 0171 383 5994

Professinal Development and Training Limited

Provides training, supervision and continuing professional
development, mainly for family lawyers.
Contact details:
Professional Development and Training Limited
20 Silbury Boulevard, Milton Keynes MK9 1L2
Tel: 01732 453227, Fax: 01732 464133

Solicitors Family Law Association (SFLA)

A national association of family solicitors which encourages a
conciliatory approach to divorce and separation. Trains members for
all issues concerning property, finance and children and provides
consultancy and other professional support.
Contact details:
SFLA, PO Box 302, Orpington BR6 8QX
Tel: 01689 850227, Fax: 01689 855833
E-mail: 106002.3040@compuserve.com

Sources of advice about mediation

Advice Services Alliance

4 Deans Court, St Paul's Churchyard, London EC4V 5AA
Tel: 0171 236 6022, Fax: 0171 248 3367, E-mail: asa@cwcom.net

Consumers' Association

2 Marylebone Road, London NW1 7DF
Tel: 0171 830 6000, Fax: 0171 830 7600, E-mail: which@which.net

Law Centres Federation

Duchess House, 18–19 Warren Street, London W1P 5DB
Tel: 0171 387 8570, Fax: 0171 387 8368
E-mail: lcf-london@dial.pipex.com

National Association of Citizens' Advice Bureaux

Myddleton House, 115–123 Pentonville Road, London N1 9LZ
Tel: 0171 833 2181, Fax: 0171 833 4362
E-mail: consultancy@nacab.org.uk

National Consumer Council

20 Grosvenor Gardens, London SW1W 0DH
Tel: 0171 730 3469, Fax: 0171 730 0191, E-mail: info@ncc.org.uk

WALES

Central Cardiff Citizens' Advice Bureau

71 Bridge Street, Cardiff CF1 2EE
Tel: 01222 398676

SCOTLAND

ACCORD, Law Society of Scotland

The ACCORD service accredits solicitors trained in mediation
techniques. It also advises parties on the suitability of their disputes
for mediation, provides assistance in getting a mediation started and
offers administrative support.

Contact details:
ACCORD
26 Drumsheugh Gardens, Edinburgh EH3 7YR
Tel: 0131 226 7411, Fax: 0131 225 2934,
E-mail: lawscot@lawscot.org.uk

Citizens' Advice Scotland

26 George Square, Edinburgh EH8 9LD
Tel: 0131 667 0156, Fax: 0131 668 4359

Scottish Consumer Council

Royal Exchange House, 100 Queen Street, Glasgow G1 3DN
Tel: 0141 226 5261, Fax 0141 221 0731, E-mail: scotconsumer.co.uk

NORTHERN IRELAND

Central Belfast Citizens' Advice Bureau

6 Callender Street, Belfast BT1 5BN
Tel: 01232 243196, Fax: 01232 312336

Central London County Court

Mediation Scheme, 13–14 Park Crescent, London WC14HT
Tel: 0171 917 5053, Fax: 0171 917 5014

Index